THE VOYAGE

OF A

VICE-CHANCELLOR

The Voyage

of a

Vice-Chancellor

CAMBRIDGE

AT THE UNIVERSITY PRESS

1919

CAMBRIDGE
UNIVERSITY PRESS

University Printing House, Cambridge CB2 8BS, United Kingdom

Cambridge University Press is part of the University of Cambridge.

It furthers the University's mission by disseminating knowledge in the pursuit of
education, learning and research at the highest international levels of excellence.

www.cambridge.org
Information on this title: www.cambridge.org/9781107511736

© Cambridge University Press 1919

This publication is in copyright. Subject to statutory exception
and to the provisions of relevant collective licensing agreements,
no reproduction of any part may take place without the written
permission of Cambridge University Press.

First published 1919
First paperback edition 2015

A catalogue record for this publication is available from the British Library

ISBN 978-1-107-51173-6 Paperback

Cambridge University Press has no responsibility for the persistence or accuracy of
URLs for external or third-party internet websites referred to in this publication,
and does not guarantee that any content on such websites is, or will remain, accurate
or appropriate.

GENTI

INTER OMNES GENTES

HOSPITIBUS

BENIGNISSIMAE

Preface

THE following extracts are from a private diary which the Author wrote whilst on an extensive tour in the United States during the autumn of 1918 as a member of the British University Mission. Our Mission had been invited to the United States by the Council of Defense at Washington and had been sent out under the auspices of the British Foreign Office. For more than sixty days we went up and down a vast country, travelling many thousands of miles, and seeing so many Universities and Colleges and so many Presidents and Professors that those amongst us who had not hitherto had the privilege of visiting the United States formed the idea that all its cities are university cities and that all the inhabitants are professors, an idea very awful to contemplate!

As the Author has tried to indicate in his Dedication, everywhere we went we met with kindness, and kindness that came from the brain as well as from the heart. But especially we owe thanks to certain "guides, philosophers, and friends" who shepherded our steps. One of these, an official of the United States Bureau of Education at Washington, accompanied us on the whole tour. His extraordinary powers of organization, his inexhaustible information, and his ready and self-sacrificing help, cannot be too highly praised. Others who helped us on our trip were: the Secretary of the Reception Committee of the Council (a professor of Harvard), who met us on our arrival at New York and accompanied us to Washington, and later to Boston; the American Secretary of the Rhodes Scholars (a professor of the Massachusetts Institute of Technology), who guided us from Boston to Chicago. From Chicago to Minneapolis we had the great advantage of the presence

of the Chairman of the Reception Committee of the American Council on Education
(a President of one of the leading Colleges
in the Middle West); and the President of
the University of Kentucky travelled with
us from St Louis to Lexington, where
his own University is situate. All these
gentlemen were ever ready and helpful in
explaining the intricacies of American
university life. We were fortunate enough
to meet them at many centres, and always
found the same helpful advice, and care for
our welfare. To each and all of them we
owe a deep debt of gratitude.

Certain chapters of this *Diary* have appeared in *Scribner's Magazine*, New York,
and others in *Country Life*, London. The
owners and editors of these monthly or
weekly publications have given the author
leave to reprint and he thanks them.

A. E. S.

St George's Day, 1919.

"It is always a writer's duty to make the world better."

DR JOHNSON.

Chapter I
THE ATLANTIC

" In the midst of this sublime and terrible storm, Dame
Partington...was seen at the door of her house,
with mop and pattens, trundling her mop, squeez-
ing out the sea-water, and vigorously pushing away
the Atlantic Ocean. The Atlantic was roused. Mrs
Partington's spirit was up; but I need not tell you
that the contest was unequal. The Atlantic Ocean
beat Mrs Partington. She was excellent at a slop,
or a puddle, but she should not have meddled with
a tempest."

SYDNEY SMITH, *Speech on the Reform Bill*,
delivered at Taunton, England, Oct. 12, 1831.

September 25th, 1918

THE present passport is pink, printed on pink paper with little red lines criss-crossing all about it. Gone—and probably gone for ever —are those aristocratic old passports with

fine lettering on fine paper, down the face
of which ran a stream of historic titles
which, in the two the Government basely
forced me to surrender in exchange for the
present pink abomination, began with a
Marquisate and trickled through the lower
degrees of the peerage until one ended in
a Barony or two, and the other fell as low
as a Baronetcy. So many historic titles
seemed to justify the "We," which reads
a little odd as, "We, Arthur James
Balfour." Each of my old passports was
studded over with "visés" and "per-
missos" and covered over with gorgeous
Russian and Turkish stamps and much
Cyrillic and Arabic script. These I had
to give up in exchange for a common-
looking paper marked by a rubber stamp in
violet-blue ink, which simply "shouted" at
the pink, with the word "seen."

The older form could be folded up and
put away in a pocket-book and forgotten
till asked for, the new form is bound up in

cheap green boards of such a size as to be always intruding on one, no matter how wide one's pockets are. The old passport had the reticence of a gentleman and was content with your signature, the new one clamours for vulgar details about your age and personal appearance, and it gets them.

The difference between passports ancient and modern may be compared with the difference between a clean £5 note, with its crisp, white paper, fine lettering and the romance of its secret signs, and that modern form of "filthy lucre" the current 10s. note.

Thursday, September 26th

We arrived at our Port of Embarkation in a gale and it continued to blow all the night, and all the next day,

Friday, September 27th

during which we wistfully tried to fulfil the divergent and incoherent instructions we had severally received from the Minister of Information: and it blew all the night of that day. On

Saturday, September 28th

it blew worse than ever and our pessimist, who is an authority on weather, cheered us up by assuring us that we were embarking at the very worst time of the year and that we should have equinoctial gales the whole way across.

It wasn't so easy to get on board. We stood in a vast, damp, dreary dock in two queues, saloon passengers and steerage passengers, and waited to have our papers inspected. Our inspector was of a slowness beyond words and when at last I was getting near to him I was so angered by a pompous man "on somebody's staff" pushing ahead of all of us and engaging in an interminable conversation with our man, that I deserted my class and joined the steerage group and was on board in five minutes. I was a little sorry that I did this as I saw a poor old Jamaican negro "turned down." Some one had told him that Jamaica was in America and he had, with a fine impartiality, registered on one paper as an American citizen and on another as a British citizen. I wonder what became of him. I suppose I shall never know.

Later in the day I had my revenge on the staff man. He turned out to be a successful writer of the more vacuous forms of *revue*, and he took his art and himself very seriously. After luncheon he changed his tunic and put on a Norfolk jacket so that down to his waist his torso or bust was civilian, whilst below his waist his lower extremities were military. In effecting this exchange something had gone wrong with his braces and all that afternoon and evening he walked about in a stately and haughty way festooned behind with loops which recalled the flowery swags of Mantegna's pictures.

Sunday, September 29th

On Sunday morning we moved from the dock into the river and waited till tea-time on its muddy and rubbish-laden waters. The wind had completely dropped and a sabbath-calm and a river-fog lay on everything. All day we waited swinging with the tide until about 5 P.M. when we felt the first delicious thrill of the engine at work. All this day large tenders laden with hundreds and hundreds of American soldiers passed us going up-stream to the City on their way from the troop-ships lying further down near the mouth of the river.

On coming on board on the previous day it became obvious that when not on deck we should be living entirely in artificial light. All windows and port-holes had been made absolutely light-proof and whilst the public saloon and state-rooms were brilliantly lit up, no ray of light was allowed to leave them. After dark the decks were quite black and if you groped on to them it was through heavy curtains and blackened doors. The insignificant glow of a cigarette was strictly forbidden and the darkness of the outside was infinitely darker than Cambridge or even Norwich at its worst.

During the morning each passenger was given a Boddy's Life Jacket and at 4 P.M. we were paraded on Deck B and received a card indicating which boat was ours, and to this we went. An officer—who ought to be a University Lecturer—then in one of the clearest, concisest and shortest of speeches told us what we were to do in case there was need to do anything. We were all wearing the life-jackets and I had thought we should feel a little self-conscious, if not ludicrous, but we didn't. It all seemed so natural, and so much in the day's work, that one took it as though one had worn such robes for years. These jackets are stuffed with the fibres known commercially as kapok. For the following account of this vegetable product I am indebted to Mr L. H. Dewey of the Bureau of Plant Industry, Washington, whose letter I quote:

The name kapok is a Malay name, applied to a cotton-like down produced in the seed pods of the kapok, or randoe, tree, *Ceiba pentandra*. This tree is native in the West Indies and in many parts of tropical America. It has been widely distributed in the Tropics of both hemispheres and is found on many of the tropical islands. In English-speaking colonies it is usually known as the silk-cotton tree. In Spanish-speaking colonies it is more often known as ceiba, though the name ceiba is often applied to other species of the genus Ceiba, and often to some of the species of the genera Bombax and Chorisia.

The kapok tree was introduced into

Java at least half a century ago, and it is cultivated there over large plantations in the region of Samarang, and is also grown along the roadsides and borders of fields on many plantations throughout the central part of the island.

During the past ten years systematic efforts have been made to set out kapok trees in plantations, and especially along roadsides, in the Philippines, and more recently in Porto Rico. These newer plantings, however, have not yet reached a stage of commercial importance.

Nearly all of the kapok of commerce hitherto has come from Java, and the greater portion of it has been handled in the markets of Rotterdam and Amsterdam, Holland.

Kapok has been used at least fifteen years as the principal material in stuffing life preservers and life belts on the Dutch steamships sailing to the Orient, and also on the North German Lloyd. I think

that it was used on the English P. & O.
Line, but I have never been on those
ships and have no definite information
on this point. It was used on the other
ships not only for life belts and life
preservers but also as a stuffing for mat-
tresses and pillows. It is a very good
salutary stuffing and serves the purpose
quite well, except that it breaks to pieces
more quickly than cotton, wool, feathers,
or hair.

Kapok has been very thoroughly tested
for buoyancy by the Government of
Holland. I think that Professor Van
Iterson, of the Hoch Schule at Delft
either planned or was interested in some
of these tests. The results indicated that
it was the most buoyant material available
for various forms of life preservers. Its
buoyancy depends on each individual
fibre. These are unicellular hairs with
relatively thin walls, practically im-
pervious to moisture, and, except under

very strong pressure, each individual cell remains very distended, like a miniature cigar-shaped balloon. In a life preserver, therefore, they act like so many millions of little sacks of air.

Kapok has been treated specially and spun experimentally at Chemnitz, Germany, but it can not be classed as a spinning fibre. It can not be spun alone without special treatment on any machinery now made. The fibres, which average scarcely more than 10 mm. in length, are not only too short for ordinary spinning material, but they lack "felting" properties necessary to make them cling together so as to form a yarn. This very lack of "felting" properties, or the property of becoming matted, makes them especially valuable as stuffing fibres. In this respect a good stuffing fibre and a good spinning fibre have qualities diametrically opposed.

After this, even when we had passed the danger-zone, we had always to carry these jackets with us and as they were white oblongs, with bold letters printed on them, when we passed one another in the inspissated gloom of the companion- or alley-ways, we looked like ghosts of newsvendors from the happy days when newspaper placards still existed. We clung to our jackets as old ladies cling to their white Shetland shawls, and, like the old ladies, we sometimes left them about.

The same fibre is used in stuffing comely waistcoats which are less conspicuous than the "Boddy Jacket," and there is also a waistcoat whose buoyancy depends on its being blown up. Opinion varied as to the relative values of these rival articles. Having both I wore both, but if I had to choose but one, I should choose the "Boddy," though the wearer should know that kapok is very inflammable. Before leaving, however, I had consulted a friend of mine, Dr P., who with his wife had just come back from the States. On the whole he spoke well of the blown-up waistcoat, at least as regards himself, but he added, "Mrs P. was not so sure as she was constantly deflating."

One elderly steward had been torpedoed seven times and after taking to the boats had been seven times rescued by the destroyers. We naturally sought the advice of so experienced an expert. "You don't 'urry Sir, you don't 'urry, there's always plenty of time," was his sole and philosophic contribution to the gentle art of being torpedoed. Another somewhat younger steward handing round tea and catching the last glimpse of land, the north-west of Ireland, calmly remarked: "Well, this is about the place they generally gets me." He had been torpedoed three out of his last four trips.

We must have crossed the bar about dinner-time, and these two words remind me that in spite of certain obvious discomforts, there were very substantial comforts on board. We had left, as we were told to do, our various ration-coupons on the dock at the port of embarkation, and crossing the gangway arrived in a ship flowing with milk and honey—a ship of sweetness and in parts of light. We were given white bread, lots of cream, real butter, Stilton cheese, sugar—even lump sugar— any amount of marmalade or jam, quantities of fruit, not only apples—if Eve had lived in 1918 I don't believe she would have wangled Adam with an apple—but grape-fruit, melons, oranges, pears, grapes, nuts, etc., etc. One couldn't help feeling with the fat boy in Pickwick, "How we shall enjoy ourselves at meals."

We dropped down the river that evening in the foggy darkness and then!

Monday, September 30th

On coming on deck on Monday I came on to one of the most glorious and fascinating scenes I have ever seen. The sun was shining brilliantly, the dancing sea was a perfect blue with glistening white caps. To the left lay Rathlin Island and the shimmering coast of Antrim, to the right Jura and Islay, a fitting and satisfying setting for the centre of the stage which was occupied by our amazing convoy. We had been told we were the largest convoy that had left our shores, but then we had been told so many things! Anyway, here in the blue sunshine and on the dancing sea was a score of great ships, and such ships! They were painted in every colour of the prism and in every variety of inconsecutive and inchoate pattern. Solomon in all his glory was not so variegated as any one of these amazing vessels, though doubtless his colour scheme was more coherent.

To explain these bizarre and dazzling things it is necessary to make a brief excursus into that manner of art known as Cubism. I do not propose to say anything about the cubist's pictures, for I never could see anything in them, but what I conceive to have happened is this: the Cubists (or perhaps the most Cubic of them) said to themselves, "There are a very large number of average, ordinary, dull people in this world who see nothing in our pictures, therefore to those people there is nothing to see and therefore to them they are invisible." When the war broke out these Cubists, who are as patriotic as they are commercially capable, said, "If to the average, ordinary, dull person our pictures are invisible, could we not by painting the British ships in our manner render them invisible, say, to the commander of a U-boat who in matters of art probably is an average, ordinary, dull individual?" At any rate the Cubists seem to have got the contract.

But however it came about we owe gratitude to some one for providing us with so radiantly beautiful a sight. At first we seemed to be moving in regular formation, keeping our distance and our time, but soon we changed the formation. We, as it were, now set to partners, we advanced towards our neighbours and then coyly (or shyly) retired; at one time it seemed to me we were playing Roger de Coverley, "up the middle and down the sides," zigzagging and pirouetting across the ocean. The whole thing was so exhilarating, so fantastic! Yet behind its grotesque and fascinating beauty —which put all the scenes of *Chu Chin Chow* or any Granville Barker scenery into the shade, for we were living, moving, vibrating—one felt such an amazing reality of Britain's power and might. A sea-plane flew over us, one of our own. I wish the Kaiser had been in it.

All this time we were encompassed about and shepherded by numerous destroyers who tore up and down on every side spying out the seas. They were not camouflaged but grey-coloured and seemed so small that one felt that if they had come within reach one could have stretched a hand over the taffrail and picked them up. We were distressed that there was no way of thanking them for their services. No more monotonous, more dangerous, more uncomfortable life is there than that led by all ratings on these convoying craft. What they do should be more fully and more publicly recognized.

In reading an unknown poet, at any rate unknown to me, the other day, I came across a poem—No. 13—whose first line so harmonised with my views about these wonder-ships that I venture to quote it:

"GLORY BE TO GOD FOR DAPPLED THINGS."

Eager to know more about one whose appreciations so happily coincided with my own views on "camouflage," I hastily turned to the note contributed by our Laureate:

Poem 13. PIED BEAUTY. Curtal Sonnet:
sprung paeonic rhythm. St Beuno's Tremeir-
chion. Summer " 77 " Autograph in A.—B
agrees.

"Faint but pursuing" for I felt I must
know at least who and when my bard was,
I turned to the author's preface. He at
least might know. Here I found that poem
number 13 is a Curtal-Sonnet

constructed in proportions resembling those of
the sonnet proper, namely 6, 4 instead of 8, 6,
with however a half line tailpiece (so that the
equation is rather $\frac{12}{2} + \frac{9}{2} = \frac{21}{2} = 10\frac{1}{2}$).

I had hoped to find the personality of a
poet, but I stumbled against what looked
like an equation of an immature algebraist.

Tuesday, October 1ˢᵗ

We closed the day in the centre of
a marine fairy scene, we awoke next
morning and found we had been dreaming.

A cold wet morning, a heavy sea, no trace of the convoy, all the ships scattered on their several occasions, the destroyers racing back to port only to turn round and start off again to escort another convoy out.

Owing to my having forgotten to put back my watch over night 55 minutes, I got up one hour before I had meant to. This vexed me quite a bit; first, because I had to live over again an hour that I had thought satisfactorily disposed of, secondly, because breakfast was not ready, and then I reflected if this mischance had happened to me in my own University, where I really ought to have been, how easily could I have reached the Senate House by 9.30 A.M. without any undue effort. About the time I should have been reading my annual address to the Members of the Senate we passed a large convoy going East.

It grew duller and rougher and for the rest of to-day, as the poet has it, "a gentle pensiveness my soul possessed."

Wednesday, October 2nd

I think the Bishop—for we have a
Bishop, and a Monsignore and a chaplain,
and several padres, a poet, an oil-man, a
play-writer, several members of the Canadian Siberian Commission, lots of flying
men and five Japanese on board—in fact
just the ordinary crowd of men (there are
only men, why aren't there children?)
whom one is used to meet on liners. The
Bishop was arguing yesterday that there
could be no news if there was no one to
read it—I think the Bishop must be an
idealist. His talk reminded me of Ronny
Knox's poem:

> There was a young man who said, God!
> It surely to you must seem odd
>> That a tree as a tree
>> Simply ceases to be
> If there's no one about in the quad.

Well, to-day we received Monday's
French and American communiqués and

we read them, so there was news—and it was good.

The Captain told us that our convoy had been attacked by U-boats but, as the modern phrase goes, there was "nothing doing." The news that we had been attacked so cheered our pessimist that he had an extra course at lunch.

Thursday, October 3rd

The worst of travelling in a boat primarily designed for freight, and which is carrying no freight—we had barely a hundred tons on board—is that the thing becomes light-headed. There was a heavy swell, and all Wednesday night and all to-day we have bobbed about in a most outrageous manner. Still to-day the sun is shining. I have a great sympathy with those folk who worship the sun. We sighted a ship and immediately turned and fled north. Evidently the neighbourhood of ships in these waters is unhealthy.

About the fourth day, from the upper deck or the ship's bow, we begin to see floating patches of seaweed—gulfweed, or sargasso (*Sargassum bacciferum*), as it is called. For the most part this appears as single stems or in small rounded heads, yellow-brown or olive-green, awash with the surface. But, as we proceed southward, larger masses appear.

William Beebe gives the following account of the gulfweed in *The Atlantic Monthly* (October, 1918, p. 477):

An amazing amount of fiction and nonsense has been written about the sargasso-weed, but the truth is actually more unbelievable. Though we see it in such immense patches, and although for days the ocean may be flecked with the scattered heads of the weed, yet it is no more at home in mid-ocean than the falling leaves in autumn may claim as

their place of abode the breeze which
whirls them about, or the moss upon
which at last they come to rest. Along
the coast of Central America the sargasso-
weed grows, on coral and rock and shell,
and flowering and fruiting after its lowly
fashion. The berry-like bladders with
which the stems are strung are filled with
gas, and enable the plants to maintain
their position regardless of the state of
the tide. Vast quantities are torn away
by the waves and drift out to sea, and
these stray masses are what we see on
every trip south, which, caught in the
great mid-ocean eddy, form the so-
called Sargasso Sea.

The weed along the coast is honest
growth, with promise of permanence.
The great floating Sargasso Sea is per-
manent only in appearance; and when
finally the big masses drift, with all their
lesser attendant freight, into the Gulf
Stream, then life becomes a sham. There

can be no more fruiting or sustained
development of gas-filled berries. No
eggs of fish or crabs will hatch, no new
generation of sea-horses or mollusks
appear among the stems. Bravely the
fronds float along; day by day the
hundred little lives breathe and feed and
cling to their drifting home. But soon
the gas-berries decay, and the frond
sinks lower and lower; as the current
flows northward, and the water becomes
cooler, the crabs move less rapidly, the
fish nibble less eagerly at the bits of
passing food. Soon a sea-horse lets go,
and falls slowly downward, to be snapped
up at once, or to sink steadily into the
eternal dusk and black night of deeper
fathoms. Soon the plant follows and,
like all its chilled pensioners, dies. The
supply from the Sargasso Sea seems unfailing, but one's sympathies are touched
by these little assemblages, so teeming
with the hope of life, all doomed by the

current which is at once their support, their breath, and their kismet.

Friday, October 4th

Wet, warm, with a sticky moisture, and still very rough. I think this day we must have passed through a cyclone. About luncheon time the sea and the wind simply seemed to lose all control over themselves. They raged like the heathen, and we tossed and pitched more than ever. At dinner-time things began to improve and for some three hours it was merely rough, then the whole thing began over again and half the night or more was a pandemonium of noise and turmoil.

Saturday, October 5th

The sea is still very rough, but the air is dry and the sun shines. This is an immense improvement and the berths are

beginning to give up their dead. They say
we are south of the Newfoundland Banks.
Sea-weed is again drifting about, probably
on its long journey from the Sargasso Sea.

In the afternoon we saw a balk of timber
slithering up and down the climbing waves.
It filled me with a sense of unutterable
loneliness. What was it doing in this limit-
less waste of waters? Whence had it come?
Whither was it going? Why? What would
be its future? Probably months of restless
tossing accompanied by an ever-increasing
water-loggedness until it slowly sinks to the
abysmal bosom of the "benthos" to form
a resting-place for deep-sea barnacles to
nestle on and a shelter under which
chaetopods can creep.

Sunday, October 6th

The weather is worthy of the day,
warm, without winds, brilliant sunshine and
a low, slow swell. We passed a Belgian relief

ship so beautifully *camouflagé* that it looked twice as far off as the Captain said it was.

Morning service (Matins) was at 10.30. Acting on the dictum of the Bishop that the only pleasure in life that never palls is stopping away from Sunday morning church, I stopped away and went on with my writing, but I was represented at the service by the Boy who also acted as organist and played "God Save the King" and three hymns. Cuthbert, who wasn't feeling quite up to it, also stayed away. He has not been down to a meal since we left the river of the port of embarkation!

In the afternoon the washing came back. The shortage of starch, which has so agitated the Episcopal Bench at home, is evidently not felt in this wonderful ship.

Monday, October 7th

All night it has been stiflingly hot and as we must not open a port-hole it has been rather oppressive. At six o'clock it suddenly began to blow, quite suddenly and with a noise like the opening of an exhaust pipe. The steward informs us that the sky is full of "mouse's tails," a cryptic but ominous utterance.

The Captain—we don't see much of the Captain—told us that he had had to cut off ten feet of the distal end of his masts in order that his ship may pass under the Grand Trunk and Intercolonial Railway Bridge, which is at last in position above Quebec. I am not an expert on masts and they look to me very well as they are, but he evidently resents his loss and has a bit of a grudge against the Railway Companies.

Every morning I read a daily portion of Professor G. E. Maclean's excellent *Studies in Higher Education in England and Scotland*. I was pleased this morning to come across the following lines:

The duties of the Vice-Chancellor at Oxford and Cambridge are so numerous and complex that it is not unusual for his health to break down, though his term of office is only two or four years.

" There is probably during term time no more harder worked official in the United Kingdom."

I wish I did not feel so well!

Tuesday, October 8th

A very rough night, the screw constantly racing out of the water and jarring one out of one's sleep. To those who like myself sleep very slowly this was a bit of a nuisance, but joy came in the morning. At sunrise the turmoil abated and we 'had a day of brilliant sunshine, tempered by a cool, north-easterly breeze.

This morning we got Cuthbert on deck and he sat in the Bishop's deck chair for some hours. I think the sun and the fresh air did him good. He is certainly eating better.

Wednesday, October 9th

Coming up towards Sandy Hook on a perfectly placid sea we were blessed with just that amount of haze which turned Coney Island into Venice, the sea into an Adriatic lagoon. We might have left Trieste overnight! The same merciful mist changed the clear-cut outlines of the sky-scrapers into Turner's pictures, and the Boy and the Poet became ecstatic with the ecstasy of youth. On landing, the joy of Cuthbert and the Boy on being again on "terra firma," for New York is built on bed rock —a very sustaining form of Gneiss, known as Manhattan Gneiss, capable of bearing great burdens or what would the sky-scrapers do, poor things?—was so great that they waltzed along the dock until they reached their respective initials and awaited with such patience as they could command the official visits of the officers of the Customs.

Everything was made easy for us and that evening we began the series of ceaseless kindlinesses and unbounded hospitalities which continued all our trip.

Chapter II

THE STATES

"If 'these' two creatures grew into one
They would do more than the world has done."
BROWNING, *The Flight of the Duchess*.

Thursday, October 10th

LAST night it was broken to me, in the kindest possible way, in sympathetic terms which could not be more "tenderer," if we may quote Mr Weller Senior, that I am to be painted for the Harvard Club. This morning I gave the first sitting at a charming studio in Gramercy Park. I am not one

who usually laughs much before noon,
but the artist was so amusing and so
bright that we hardly quit laughing from
9 to 11 A.M. The studio is decorated by a
portrait on a large scale of the four Harvard
Professors of Philosophy, Royce, Wm.
James, Parker and Münsterberg. The last-
named is represented by an empty chair.
It seems that his habitual insolence and
" overbearichkeit " was a bit more than the
artistic temperament could stand. After
a few sittings he was asked to leave the
studio and to stay away.

The following is queer but true. When
it became clear that the United States were
about to enter the war, Münsterberg
petitioned the authorities to intern him—
one wishes one could spell it without the
" n "—in the Cambridge gaol, as he thought
that there his food supply, always an
important item in a German's outlook,
could be more generously supplemented
than elsewhere.

We dined at the Century Club with its members and made speeches.

Friday, October 11th

Raising the liberty loan has clothed Fifth Avenue in a mass of bunting, each section being devoted to one of the Allies. The effect is very brilliant as the flags flutter in the sunny, clear breeze.

Cuthbert is very much disappointed that he did not arrive in time to assist at the unveiling of the heroic bronze statue of Mr Chauncey M. Depew, which the ex-Senator has presented to his native town. Mr Depew delivered the unveiling and unfailing dedicatory oration. The advantage of these proceedings is obvious. There will be for instance no need now to get together a Chauncey M. Depew Memorial Committee. No one will have to equate in terms of cash the nicely balanced more or less of his esteem for the ex-Senator, with his duty to the Liberty Loan. That perennial source of difference, marble, bronze or lead is eliminated. Bronze it is, and bronze is as durable as brass. Mr Chauncey M. Depew pronounced the eulogy himself, and no one could have done it better. A man, even a politician, is very conscious of his own virtues and no ex-Senator can be charged with that lack of appreciation of the subject of his memorial statue which is often met with in unveiling orations on post-mortem inaugurations. We shared Cuthbert's disappointment.

Dined with the members of Harvard University at their splendid Club and made speeches.

Saturday, October 12th

To-day, being Liberty Day, Mr Wilson put on a black coat and a top-hat and marched with an interminable pro-

cession down Fifth Avenue. I saw it soon
after 11 A.M. and again about 4 P.M. and
for all I know it may still be marching. The
whole thing was impressive, but the " moment " was the passing of the President
carrying a small flag. One could not help
reflecting on the power of good it would do
if the Pope would put on a black coat and
a top-hat and walk down the Corso. Such
things seem to bring folk together.

Dined with the New York Schoolmasters
at the Aldine Club, down-town, and made
speeches. After dinner went to the Auditorium, away up-town, and made more
speeches. At 5.30 P.M. on this day there
was not in this Continent a soul more keen
about Liberty than I was, but by 10.30 P.M.
I had weakened quite a bit. I had listened
to eighteen speeches on the subject and
delivered two. I sympathized with Patrick
Henry who exclaimed after marrying his
fourth wife, "Give me Liberty or give me
Death, I prefer Death."

Sunday, October 13th

Motored some forty miles up the Hudson, a brilliant day in all senses. Dined with the Rhodes Scholars at the Harvard Club and made speeches.

Monday, October 14th

As our newspapers say when the House of Commons has an all-night session, I am "still sitting" to my artist. I took Cuthbert to see her and the two got on very well together. We left in the afternoon for Washington and dined on the train. We made no speeches.

Tuesday, October 15th

During the afternoon, President Wilson received us and very cordially asked us to lunch on Thursday, October 17th. After leaving him we spent a couple of hours

with Bishop Shane at the Roman Catholic
University where amongst many things we
saw was a fully equipped and entirely
modern Chemical Laboratory, as large or
almost as large as any in Great Britain.
In this worked monks and priests of most
of the religious orders

Wednesday, October 16th

After a Conference on Education in
the morning with the authorities of the
War Department we embarked on the
Admiralty yacht *Sybil* and left for Mount
Vernon. It was a perfect autumn afternoon
and the brilliancy of the fading autumn
leaves was reflected in the still waters of the
Potomac. Their colours were so blended
that we could only wonder at the beauty
of the scene, but our hosts were by no
means satisfied. They apologized for the
absence of certain red tints, this they at-
tributed to a cold spell in September which

had caused the fading foliage to skip one stage in its colour *diminuendo*. As has been pointed out, "there's beauty in the colour of decay," but it was obvious that there is more beauty if the decay be gradual and not unduly hastened by cold spells.

As we came opposite to Washington's house, the flag was lowered, a bell tolled and the ship's bugler sounded the "Last Post." A naval officer on the *Sybil* told me that this touching tribute to a great gentleman dated back to 1812 when the British Admiral of a fleet sent to fight Washington's countrymen, as his ships passed Mount Vernon on their way up the Potomac to shell the Federal Capital, gave the order to salute the grave of the first President with this usage, which has ever after been followed. Well, sailors always were gentlemen[1].

The charm of the house, of the garden, of the several views both inland and river-

[1] Germans alone excepted.

wards was multiplied by the beauty of the afternoon, and we left as sundown was setting in, with buzzards circling over us and a solitary blue heron standing on one leg on a grassy islet near the landing-stage.

We dined that night with the Assistant High Commissioner of our country and the only speeches were two quite short ones to explain there were to be no speeches.

Thursday, October 17th

To-day we lunched with the President and Mrs Wilson. Both were extremely cordial and friendly and did us the quite unusual honour of granting us two hours of their much occupied time. Later some of us visited the Carnegie Institute and tried to grasp the almost incredible variety of its many activities and the quite incredible number of dollars it administers.

Later in the day the Trustees of the Carnegie Institute gave a banquet at the

Washington Hotel where we met a couple of hundred of the most distinguished men in Washington. Here the speeches reached a climax, for they began with the melons. I made an after-dinner speech before the soup was served, and had to leave out quite a lot of points. Whenever the band paused for a moment some one made a speech, and there were so many, and so many of us lacked what the Railway folk call "terminal facilities" that we had well-nigh three hours of speeches. But it was all so kindly and so friendly that it won our hearts.

Friday, October 18th

This morning we went to Baltimore, and here perhaps we came across more evidence of the terrible plague which this autumn is decimating the land than we had till now met with. Hitherto I have not mentioned it, but even on the dock at New

York, the Head of the British Mission in
New York City had told us something of
the extent and virulence of the scourge, a
very fatal form of influenza followed in
many cases by a still more fatal form of
pneumonia. That very morning two of his
clerks had died. On one day there were
750 deaths from this plague in New York
City alone. The Secretary of State at
Washington had given me an appalling list
of the deaths amongst the families of the
Diplomatic Corps in Washington; no Em-
bassy, no Ministry, had escaped.

One saw in Washington folks walking
about the streets wearing white masks, something like gas-masks. In the barbers' shops
all the attendants wore masks, but the supply
of them was totally inadequate. The medical
and nursing profession, greatly depleted by
the war, practically broke down. At Baltimore, although no one spoke much about
it, we heard gruesome stories of a little girl
found shaking in a cupboard whither she had

fled after the death of both parents and all her brothers and sisters; of the bodies of a man and his wife found alone in a house eight days after their death. It was as it were living through the pages of Daniel Defoe. The day before we reached Baltimore 250, including some of the more brilliant of the young Johns Hopkins teachers, had died. At Philadelphia, with a population of something under two million, there had already been 250,000 cases. All theatres, churches, "movie-" shows, and saloons were closed. No assemblage of more than twenty-eight persons was permitted. The undertakers and the authorities at the cemeteries were unable to deal with the dreadful conditions which prevailed. Thousands of bodies lay unburied, and owing to the national feeling about funerals the people would not adopt the natural and hygienic expedient of burying their dead in cloaks or in sheets. An old friend of mine, Lady ——, told me at Washington that she had just buried her nephew in Philadelphia and had to pay £40 for a coffin which took three days to deliver.

So great was the need of help at the necropolis at Philadelphia that the Admiral in command of the shipbuilding yards at Hog Island sent over two of his excavators to dig two great common graves. After some hours he was informed that there was no one to direct his men where to dig or to register the dead or indeed to do anything. Although he made no charges, yet he found some outside person was taking money. He telephoned to the Archbishop—in America you telephone to anyone—to say that unless some one in authority took charge within two hours he would recall his excavators, and somehow something was arranged.

In the State of Connecticut the "jailbirds" were requisitioned and detailed to dig graves. The epidemic has been most fatal in the military and the naval camps. Already it has claimed a greater number of victims in the army and the navy than the total casualties in the war.

In spite of the grief and sorrow which we could not but note in our hosts' faces, they received us with a brave front. Naturally, we felt keenly that at a time of such national woe we ought not to be intruding, but perhaps after all we could do "no other" and so they and we simply "carried on" and talked on other matters.

At Baltimore we visited the new University buildings of Johns Hopkins, new since I had been there, a fine set of libraries and laboratories built of a pleasant light red brick with ample windows. There had been the usual fight between the people who were to use the buildings and the architects. Here the Professors won, for in Johns Hopkins the university rooms and windows are large and let in floods of light.

We lunched at the Country Club beside the Golf Course and made speeches. So

many speeches did we make that it was
4 P.M. before we rose to hurry off to an
interview which Cardinal Gibbons had
promised us. His Eminence was a refined
and kindly old gentleman, 84 years of age,
yet with strength and courage and truth in
his face, just the sort of saint to steady the
nerves and bring hope to the heart of a
sorely stricken and largely ignorant population. He told us that he was the youngest
prelate at the Vatican Council in 1870, and
that now he was the oldest Roman Catholic
bishop alive. He also told us that the celebrations in honour of the Jubilee of his
election to the Bench, which were just due,
had been postponed owing to the pestilence,
and somehow he gave me the impression
that he was not altogether sorry.

The Boy visited the tomb of Edgar Allan
Poe in the heart of the city, and thought it
needed care.

We were "off to Philadelphia" in the
evening.

Saturday, October 19th

Motored to the studio, in the University, of Tait Mackenzie, whose sculptures go from strength to strength. He is modelling a group of men going over the top, the finest war memorial I have yet seen. Later we visited the University Art Museum, full of beautiful things, beautifully displayed. The Museum has a circular auditorium of novel and stately proportions and with perfect acoustic properties. We lunched at Houston Hall with the faculty and made innumerable speeches. One by the Provost, a very charming Provost, contained some quite plain speaking about the way the old Universities in Great Britain had kept their doors shut to foreign students; this and further criticism after dinner, when we all spoke over again, has set us all thinking. I had hoped that in a Quaker City one would not speak unless the spirit moved one, but the "attendant spirit" in the form of the Provost was always with us and was always moving us.

In the afternoon we motored to the Quaker College of Swarthmore, a co-educational institution in which the education is by no means left out. As in other places, the buildings were set on a hill, in vast grounds, and equipped lavishly; for instance there is a large open-air theatre, a fine swimming bath and an observatory with a 24 in. lens telescope, a finer instrument than exists in Ireland, as our astronomical member told us, and many other features hard to find in a boys' or girls' College in our country.

Sunday, October 20th

Spent part of the morning at Tait Mackenzie's studio in his charming home. The Boy, who has for some days been suffering from suppressed music, obtained a certain temporary measure of relief at their grand piano.

In the afternoon we visited some dear old colonial churches in which Washington worshipped and then, by way of contrast, went to a great magnate's palace and saw the finest private collection of pictures I have ever seen. Rembrandt's "Mill," recently bought from Lord Lansdowne, hangs in the galleries. This is regarded by Bode, who has lately, we are told, been organizing the artistic looting of the invaded countries, as the most perfect picture in the world, but since he failed to distinguish a Lucas from a Leonardo, or to acknowledge his error when found out, his opinion on artistic matters leaves us unmoved.

Some Italian pictures have, owing to a certain law, a little difficulty in leaving their country. One collector who had bought at a considerable cost a genuine Old Master in Rome got over this difficulty by having a sea-scape lightly painted over it. On reaching the West the collector sent it to his picture-cleaner to have the sea-scape removed, and after some months he wrote to ask how this was getting on. The picture-cleaner replied: "We have removed the sea-scape and we have removed the Old Master and what do you wish done with 'The Coronation of William IV'?"

Monday, October 21st

This morning the Admiral in command of the shipbuilding yard at Hog Island took us over it. Fifteen months ago students from the University were botanizing on its swampy site. To-day there are some forty ships in all stages of construction, seventy miles of railway track in the yards, 30,000 workmen, who with their families are housed in hundreds of dwellings which have sprung from the sea-foam in the course of a few months. There are numerous hotels and clubs for the unmarried hands.

Here we met a camouflager, who allowed, as I had seen in New York, that much more blue is used on their ships than on ours. He also told us that the design was by no means haphazard, but carefully thought out and drawn on paper before being adopted. Each ship had a model and unless the camouflage succeeded in deceiving the enemy by a certain number of points in the compass—I suppose the Censor won't let me say how many—it was rejected altogether or revised.

Later in the morning we motored to Bryn Mawr which was as charming as ever. Here we lunched and then went on to Haverford, an old home of mine, which like the Brown University at Providence, R.I., and doubtless others, has rejected the gilded unsectarianism of Mr Carnegie.

We dined at the Arts Club with the Director of the Drexel Institution, who had the happy idea of asking each of us to talk about ourselves. Never have I heard better speeches!

Tuesday, October 22nd

We had a quiet day at Princeton, a really restful one. In the morning we visited some of the numerous departments turned into war work, especially those connected with aircraft, for Princeton has specialized in this branch. After an informal lunch with my host at my old Princeton home, we had two hours to ourselves, a great boon in these hurried days. Then we attended a Review, the President taking the salute, and afterwards a short formal meeting in Nassau Hall with the Faculty. This was a very dignified proceeding. The speeches were short and to the point.

It was a memorable occasion. Fifty years ago, to the day, President McCosh, whose name you can still conjure with, took over the guidance of what was then a much smaller institution. Five years ago to the day I had the honour of taking part in the opening exercises of Dean West's magnificent Graduate College, now the home of the Paymasters of the Fleet. But these anniversaries are as nothing compared to the fact that over the Hall in which we met the British flag was floating where it had not floated for 177 years!

Wednesday, October 23rd

On passing through New York we were entertained at a most sumptuous banquet by the members of the Lotus Club. Here we met many of the outstanding men of the City, in all branches of literature, learning and commerce, and here we heard the last of the many Wilson notes. As so often happens, the evening report was an exaggeration of what the morrow was to bring forth. Much eloquence, for the speeches with one exception (and the speaker of this sat next me) were long and many, dealt at length on the term "unconditional" but that word was lacking in the full report of the President's Note in the newspapers next morning.

The third of the classical injunctions to the after-dinner speaker "Get up, get on and get down" is neglected in this country. Never have I heard so many brilliant perorations passed by—especially by one of our Mission—and the first always seemed to me the best. Nevertheless it was a most successful gathering and we left a little before midnight much heartened by innumerable expressions of good-will and much touched by innumerable acts of kindness.

Thursday, October 24th

Our visit to Yale was another restful one. In the two laboratories I visited, the pathological and the biological, I was impressed both by the thoroughness and by the originality of the researches being carried on. Here, as at other American universities, there is ample room and a most cordial welcome awaiting the British graduate who wishes to study on lines hitherto hardly touched on in our Islands.

Friday, October 25th

The President of Yale had in the most kindly fashion arranged a short conference between the Faculty and the members of the Commission; this my colleagues tell me was one of the most helpful meetings which had as yet taken place; unfortunately before it was more than half-way through I more or less collapsed. The incessant strain of meeting hundreds of hospitable hosts each day, the constant speeches and the eternal lack of sleep had proved too much for more than one of us. I retired to the handsome library of the comfortable club which put us up, a library where that blessed word "SILENCE" is not only enjoined but exercised, and fell asleep in an arm-chair. On waking I decided, to my great regret, to omit Amherst, Smith and other Colleges, and go straight to Boston. Here I took refuge with an old Cambridge friend in the quietest of hotels inhabited by great numbers of dear old mid-Victorian ladies whose age justifies the proud boast of the proprietor that no one ever dies in his hotel. On arrival I went to bed.

Saturday, October 26th

Slept.

Sunday, October 27th

Slept most of the morning and in the afternoon went out to the hospitable house of the President of Harvard. On the

way our most kindly guide and his wife
drove us out to Concord through autumn-
tinted roads and country lanes. We saw the
homes of Hawthorne and Emerson. It was
interesting to learn that the son of the latter,
Dr Edward Emerson, was still living in his
father's village, just as it is to know that
Longfellow's daughter is still living in her
father's stately house in Cambridge just
around the corner from President Lowell's
house. We saw the virile statue by a
Concord sculptor of the young farmer who
fired the first shot in the War of Rebellion
standing at the foot of the bridge inscribed
with these lines:

> By the rude bridge that arched the flood
> Their flag to April's breeze unfurled
> Here once the embattled farmers stood
> And fired the shot heard round the world.
>
> April 19th, 1775.

We also saw on what was once the battle-
field of Concord a touching tribute to our
soldiers:

They came three thousand miles and died,
To keep the past upon its throne
Unheard beyond the ocean tide
Their English Mother made her moan.

April 19th, 1775.

On the way home we stopped at the
old cemetery at Sleepy Hollow where in
ideal setting Emerson and Hawthorne and
Thoreau lie. The sun was setting, a light
autumn mist veiled all sharp outlines; it was
four-thirty on a Sunday afternoon, a time
when one's vitality is at its lowest, a time
when at home I always read Thomson's
City of Dreadful Night. I felt at peace with
the world and in complete harmony with
tombs.

Monday, October 28th

Early in the morning we visited
Tufts College, pleasantly set on a hill. At
11 A.M. I lectured to some 700 Harvard
students in khaki and naval kit on some of

the inconveniences they may meet at the front. Nobody coughed!

The great crowds of splendid youths we meet everywhere seem almost overwhelming, full of fun, working hard and deadly in earnest. At least half of them everywhere are in sailor's uniform and are apparently in training for commissions, though how such thousands are to find ships is difficult to imagine. Of course, many of them are specializing in such subjects as sea-planes, wireless, etc.

Tuesday, October 29th

This morning we visited Boston College, a Jesuit College, which grants degrees. As usual the buildings are placed on a hill commanding beautiful views of river, lake, mountain and city, the outline of the last-named tempered by distance. All this we saw from a roof-garden. On descending in the elevator I noticed with envy that it was fitted with a mechanism, which, if Mr Edison could but fit it on all politicians, orators and after-dinner speakers, would save an immense amount of time and enable us to get on with the war. The mechanism enables the lift to record: "This elevator automatically closes itself within 30 seconds."

The chapel, and indeed all the buildings, were stately, well proportioned and satisfying to the eye. The inside decorations were exceptionally beautiful and some of the more artistic and restful were the work of one of the Fathers. An elderly priest seemed to take an especial and solicitous interest in me, and after a time he confided in me that though he had met many Oxford men I was the first Cambridge man he had ever seen. He watched over me as if I was an unique specimen and before we left gave me to understand that this singular experience had greatly widened his outlook on life.

{ 62 }

On the way home I was pleased to find that the President was using and had used for years the *Cambridge Pocket Diary*. As the originator, and for some years the author, of that modest tome I felt a certain degree of pride.

We lunched with the President of "Tech" and his wife in the magnificent new buildings which have been put up on the Cambridge side of the Charles River since I was last in Boston.

During the afternoon we met the Harvard Faculty in their Hall and had many helpful talks.

After dinner we went into Boston to a reception at the new home of the American Academy of Science. Here again I met many old friends. One, a world-wide authority on Brachiopods and Japanese art, who had been very good to me over thirty years ago when first I came to Boston, had travelled sixty miles to see me again. The crowd, however, was so great and the noise we

made was so loud we could converse but
little. One felt in sympathy with the old
lady who said "How can one converse if
people will talk?" However, I was lucky
enough to meet several zoologists and we
got away into a quiet corner and talked
shop.

Wednesday, October 30th

Yesterday it was 80 degrees in the
shade and at 8 A.M. this morning it was
already 70 degrees. The heat is indeed
overwhelming. We are assured it is unusual, but except in the Tropics the weather
seems to me to be always and everywhere
unusual.

The wife of our host took us to see
"The House of the Seven Gables" at
Salem. This is a delightful place and is
maintained with the same pious and thought-
ful care as is Mount Vernon. The whole
arrangement recalled the merchants' houses

at King's Lynn, for behind the house is a garden running down to the water's edge where the schooners used to anchor, and in the garden is a counting-house.

The headlines of the newspapers are as large as ever but not so quaintly phrased. However, I have just come across an old copy of a southern journal which records the capture of Nazareth in the following words:

"British capture Christ's Home Town."

Another one which heralded an interview with one of our Mission was:

"DISHPAN loses lure for female sex in England, says prominent British Woman Educator."

We left in the evening for Montreal, travelling luxuriously in a private car which had been kindly placed at our service by the Dominion Government.

Thursday, October 31ˢᵗ

All Hallowe'en.

At Montreal we were received by the
President and Faculty of McGill University
in their spacious Library. Here we were
shewn their admirable system of card-
cataloguing, and the rapidity with which a
book asked for can be placed in the asker's
hands. One feature that struck us greatly
was their circulating library. Hundreds of
books are sent to country villages in batches
of a dozen or so, and are sent back after a
certain fixed period. It recalled the same
sort of distribution that exists in our Local
Lectures organizations in England, but it is
carried out on a greater scale. Canada does
everything she can to help the farmers and
their women-folk in far away districts, and the
Post-Office carries for them, free of charge,
any weekly newspaper they care to order.

McGill University, though sadly depleted by the absence of a very large

percentage of its members at the war, was still keeping the flag of learning flying. We lunched with the President of the University and his wife, and met many of the leading Professors. Nothing could have been kinder than our reception. It is thirty-two years ago since I first visited this great Canadian University, and the changes and improvements that have been effected in that time are truly remarkable.

Later in the day we visited the Town Fine Art Museums and some private collections. A former pupil of mine is doing a great work in Montreal in getting together and admirably setting out great and varied collections of artistic objects. Like so many students of the biological sciences he has a real feeling for colour, form and design.

We dined with the Governors of McGill University at the University Club. We made speeches and enjoyed short talks with many old friends.

Friday, November 1st

All Saints' Day.

In the morning some of us visited the Macdonald College of Agriculture near St Anne's, a very efficient and as usual most beautifully equipped institution. In the afternoon we went to three of the buildings amongst the dozen which, scattered about in the City and French quarter of the City, constitute the Montreal and Roman Catholic University of Laval. A second half of this great institution is in Quebec and just at present there is a movement on foot to separate one from the other. We saw the Schools of Commerce, of Veterinary Science, and of Dentistry. The students of the last two Schools have proved invaluable in France, and have taken a very full and most helpful share at the Front.

At Laval the lectures are in French and it is primarily, though not exclusively, the University of the French Canadian. McGill students attend some of the Laval Courses, especially Law Courses.

In the evening the Boy and I dined with one or two of the big men in Montreal and listened to some very lively comments as to the men in the Dominions the British Government "delighted to honour." I tried to assure them that the Dominion did not suffer alone.

Saturday, November 2nd

We left early for Ottawa, arriving at that "proud city of the Waters" soon after noon. The Governor-General gave us lunch at the new and magnificent Château Laurier Hotel and here we met the Premier, upon whom I had conferred the honorary degree of LL.D. less than five months ago. Laurier and many of the present Cabinet Ministers were there but there were few speeches.

I spent some time at the headquarters

of the Entomological Branch of the Department of Agriculture. With its twelve
accessory laboratories scattered throughout
Canada it is doing great work second to
none in or out of Canada. We had tea
with the Duke and Duchess at Rideau
Hall, dinner at the Golf Club where Bishop,
the Canadian "ace," was also dining, a
truly marvellous airman who has brought
down fifty Huns.

Sunday, November 3rd

Reached Toronto quite early in the
morning after a somewhat chequered night.
I spent most of the day with the mothers
and friends of some of the Canadian
officers who had stayed during the last four
years at my Lodge.

We had tea at the house of one of the
leading financial authorities of the country
who is however more proud of the beauty
of his Bank's banknotes than of his out-

standing business ability. He thinks they will live and certainly they ought to. To most folk the beauty of a banknote is in direct proportion to the dominant cypher and they seldom look beyond this, yet they should dwell on the charm of the portrait of Martha Washington on some of the U.S. issues.

Monday, November 4th

This was really a great day for us. We saw something of the magnificent buildings of the university with their complete equipment in every department. We had a helpful talk with the Faculty and learned much about the largest and wealthiest of the great Canadian Universities. Toronto is co-educational. They have the most absolute and the fullest equality of the sexes and the women have the front seats in the lecture rooms.

As I have written we really had a great

day: most of us managed to get in four speeches.

(i) In the morning we addressed the Faculty on the objects and aims of the Mission; here as indeed everywhere we were welcomed and made to feel welcome.

(ii) A little after noon we lunched with several hundred of the leading business men at the Empire Club, and here an unfortunate thing happened. In my speech I described how one of the less informed of our Labour Members had reproached the older Universities for neglecting to teach what he called "the newer subjects," such as Textile-Fabrics, Brewing and Dyeing. In replying to him I had pointed out that these subjects were by no means new, that textile-fabrics had begun to come into use in the Garden of Eden, that the processes of fermentation were understood by Noah, and that dyeing was one of the most ancient of arts. In reporting this part of my speech the newspapers made me say that "dying was one of the oldest of human industries." I was sorry for this, as though the undertakers seemed pleased I fear the local clergy thought me flippant.

(iii) Immediately after lunch we were received by the Mayor and made speeches to the Corporation. The Mayor was kindness itself, and showered us with gifts, culminating in lovely silken Canadian flags.

(iv) We dined at a charming club as the guests of the University. I sat between the Governor and the Premier of the Province, and here we were delighted by meeting again the unveiler of the recently erected statue to Lincoln at Springfield, Ill. We all made speeches.

The food conditions in Canada are to a visitor from the other side of the Atlantic overwhelming. They are the same in the United States. The people of North America have made great and, for the most part, voluntary sacrifices to solve the food problem in Europe, and they have solved

it. Much more would they send could they
get it across. Still much remains behind.

At the numerous hospitable dinners and
banquets we had eaten the fare was both
ample and excellent, but the excess of a
City Dinner was mercifully and properly
absent. At the hotels things were on a
different basis. At Toronto we were housed
in a thoroughly comfortable house, not one
of those gilded palaces one finds in New
York, but one which provided everything
we could want, and here is a list of the
things we could eat:

Blue Point Oysters, Malapeque Oysters 45[1], Cocktail 50;
Cotuit Oysters 50, Bread and Butter 10.

Crabflakes Cocktail 60, Shrimps Cocktail 60, Lobster Cocktail 75, Oyster Stew 30, with cream 40.

HORS D'ŒUVRE: Romanoff Caviar on Ice 1.25, Grape
Fruit 30, Celery 35, Salted Almonds 30, Chow Chow 30,
Bengal Chutney 30, Dill Pickles 20, French Sardines
in oil 50, Olives 30, Stuffed Celery 50, Chili Sauce 10,
Chutney 15, Grape Fruit Suprême 60, Anchovies in
Oil 60.

SOUP: Consommé Japonais 30, Crème of Chicken 35, Potage
Milanais 30, Hot or cold Consommé, clear 30,

[1] The figures indicate cents.

garnished 35, Chicken Broth clear 30, with chicken and rice 35, Celery Broth 30, Clam Broth 30, Mock Turtle 35, Purée of Split Pea 30, Mongole Soup 30, Onion Soup au Gratin 35, Onion Soup in cream 33.

All strained soups in cups.

FISH: Boiled Fresh Codfish, egg sauce 70, Lobster and Finnan Haddie Newbourg 90, Boiled Jumbo Whitefish hôtelière 70, Fried Green Smelts with bacon, tartare 70, (15 Minutes), Planked Whitefish with cucumbers 75, Cold Lobster mayonnaise 80–1.50.

SPECIALS: Lamb Chops sauté champvallon 85, Breaded milk-fed Chicken Maryland 1.25, Braised Premium Ham mashed Sweet Potatoes 90, Boiled Lamb Steak Foyot 1.15, Calf head en Tortue 80, Cold Sliced Capon and Tongue Asparagus Tips 1.00, Omelette Célestine 65.

ROASTS: Roast Lamb Mint Sauce 85, Roast Turkey Cranberry Sauce 1.10, Roast Ribs of Beef au Jus 75.

VEGETABLES: Cauliflower Mousseline 35, Potato Marquis 30, New Bermuda Potato in cream 30, Boiled 15, Baked Potato 25, Mashed Potatoes 20, Creamed Potatoes 30, Beets in butter 30, Succotash 30, Stewed Tomatoes 35, French fried 25, California asparagus 35.

COLD CUTS: Roast Lamb 80, Chicken (Half) 1.00, Sliced Capon argentine 90, Lamb tongue 60, Beef tongue 70 Sliced Turkey 90.

SALADS: Shrimp 80, Tomatoes 35, Lobster 1.00, Fruit 60, Chicken 60, Hearts of Lettuce 35, Lettuce and Tomato 40, Cucumber 35, Watercress 30, Russian dressing 15, Mayonnaise dressing 15, Roquefort dressing 30.

ICE CREAM AND ICES: Strawberry Ice Cream 30, Orange

Water Ice 25, Neapolitaine 35, Chocolat Parfait 35, Coffee Ice Cream 30, Vanilla 30, Chocolate 30, Café Parfait 35, Lemon Water Ice 35.

FRUITS AND PRESERVES: Honey Dew Melon 35, Grape Fruit 30, Banana 15, Assorted Fruits 50, Red Currant Jelly 35, Bar-le-Duc 40, Canton Ginger 30, Orange 30.

CHEESE: Richelieu 20, McLaren's imperial 20, Neuf-châtel 20, Canadian 20, Camembert 30, Roquefort 40, Swiss 30, Ingersoll cream 20.

COFFEE: Coffee with cream, small pot for one 20, large pot 40, Demi-Tasse 10, with cream 15, Ice Coffee 20, Cocoa, Chocolate 25, Ice Tea with cream 20, Horlick's Malted Milk 20, Milk per bottle 10.

++·++·++·++·++

Dishes not on menu will be served by request.

++·++·++·++·++

"All persons in ordering food ought to consider the needs of Great Britain and the Allies for wheat, beef, bacon and food, and that the Canada Food Board desires the public to do everything in their power to make these commodities available for export by eating as little as possible of them, and by making use of substitutes and avoiding waste."

Tuesday, November 5th

We went to bed this morning before 1 A.M. and got up at 6.30 to start for Niagara. We had, as ever, perfect weather and many picturesque views of streams, lakes, and woods. Hitherto I have always visited Niagara from the American side and this is, I think, the better way. Coming first to the Canadian side the views are less impressive.

The falls are much as they were and do not seem to have changed in the last two-and-thirty years. The Victoria Park on the Canadian side, the park on the American side and on Goat Island and the new hotels have, however, vastly improved the amenity of the " section." On the other hand, the factories, power houses, etc., which desecrate the cliffs between the Falls and the Rapids, grow in number and in horror.

We left in the late afternoon for Windsor and here we had to leave our Canadian private car. Those of us, however, who had comfortable beds could not tear ourselves from the Canadian soil and remained in the car. The rest of us continued in the train which embarked on a ferry, the ferry crossed the Detroit River and at 2 A.M. we were at rest in one of the most comfortable of the many comfortable hotels we lodged at during our tour.

Wednesday, November 6th

Some of our party got up early and visited Mr Ford's works. I did not. After all, they did not see the works, but heard quite a lot about them from one of the chief managers. The works are on a large scale and the workmen receive a minimum of £1 a day. In addition to this their morals are carefully scrutinized. A woman cannot give her husband a black eye without Mr Ford being 'phoned up, and he at once adjusts the domestic difference. The number of workmen is about 50,000 and the daily pay-bill amounts to at least £50,000.

Mr Ford is now out to win the war and

has quite voluntarily and unostentatiously cut down his own income to what must be an almost starvation rate for a multi-millionaire; I forget to how many hundred thousand pounds he reduced his annual income.

Mid-day we left for Ann Arbor and here we spent a delightful four-and-twenty hours. One of the most inspiring sights we had seen was the march past of some two or three thousand students in khaki and in sailors' kit. They were simply splendid as they moved to the tune of the Michigan march familiar to our ears through Sousa's Band. Ann Arbor is the oldest and most renowned of the State Universities in the Middle West, and it was with peculiar pleasure and pride that we received at the hands of the genial and friendly President the distinction of Honorary Degrees. The ceremony was simple and very dignified. We were each presented in short, but graceful, speeches by the Professor of Philosophy spoken in

English. Latin would have saved many of
our blushes.

I was interested to learn that the
University employs five "whole-time"
doctors to look after the health of the
students. For the payment of $5 a year
each student receives free medical attend-
ance, free medicine and free treatment at
one of the University hospitals. Ann Arbor
has a very large medical school.

Thursday, November 7th

We are living altogether too fast and
I doubt whether we can stand the strain,
so many things happen and all at once.
The barber told me this morning that Ohio
had gone wet or dry, I forget which, but
as we go all round, but not into, Ohio
it does not much matter. These constant
and sudden changes in the humidity of large
tracts of land must of course affect the
conditions of a large section of the popula-

tion, but in what way is a matter of dispute. Russia went dry about three years ago, but the Muscovite millennium still tarries.

Then they say Mr Ford is not elected Senator; yet he had a lot in his favour—unlimited and moral workmen, innumerable motor-cars, and he is, they tell me, a republican on a democratic ticket; "carrying water on both shoulders," as they say here. In our country such arguments would have proved irresistible.

A son has been born to the chauffeur of our host. He is radiant and quite unresponsive to talks of armistice. To him, if he clearly understands what it is, an armistice seems a long way off and very intangible, whilst he can see and hear, and if his wife will let him, touch his little babe.

Then as a climax, "Peace" was declared at about 1.30 P.M. Ann Arbor is a small place and took the news calmly. The corner boy, almost an extinct mammal, continued to decorate his corner undismayed. But it was otherwise on the train. Passengers from Detroit told us that all work had ceased, all the factories had emptied, all the whistles and hooters were whistling and hooting, and all the flags were flying. The news seemed so overwhelming that it interfered with reason. Of course, Peace couldn't and didn't come like this, but the only one on the train who showed a reasonable appreciation of events was the elderly conductor who said to me in an inimitable drawl: "Yes, sir, we're celebrating the news of Peace on every section of this line, *but it ain't confirmed.*"

At Kalamazoo we were joined by three beautifully dressed ladies. On hearing the news they had hurried into their most splendid creations and their most ravishing toques and were on their way to join in the peace celebration in Chicago, which they opined would be on a great scale. When some kindly Professors boarded the train and told us that the news was, to say the least, premature, we gently broke it to the ladies. They showed no disappointment and little surprise, indeed they laughed merrily. So great is the moral effect of really beautiful clothes and so sustaining is the consciousness of being the best dressed women in the crowd! It affords a striking example of the triumph of matter over mind.

The kindness of our hosts—and to us the whole nation seem to be our hosts—is inexhaustible. Everywhere we go we are expected and helped through. The very custom's houses open their doors for us and the Revenue officers won't even glance at our luggage. The railway authorities had sent to our train to help us on our way to Chicago a very able and really interesting young official who was courtesy itself. He told us that but a few years ago he had been in an orchestra where he played the drum. I am fortunately immune to music, but it sticks in my mind that Dan Godfrey once told me that he who plays the drum must have a great sense for, and appreciation of, "time."

This quality may account for the rapid
career of our friend in the Railway World.
I hope he will in time rise to be President
of the Line. I am sure he would be a good
one.

We arrived in Chicago in a deluge of
rain and saw what remained of the celebration. We were soon housed in the luxurious
and comfortable University Club and "so
to bed."

Friday, November 8th

We spent to-day at the University of
Chicago. This is one of the youngest, one
of the most original of the United States
Universities. Youth accounts for much of
this originality, President Harper—he was
President of Chicago when first I visited
it—accounted for more. Youth is also
responsible for the fact that though at other
centres there may be single edifices more
stately and more beautiful than any at

Chicago, it is, as regards its buildings, one of the most complete and most uniform of all American Universities. Like the Unities of the Drama, as expounded by Mr Curdle to Nicholas Nickleby, it combines "a completeness—a kind of universal dovetailedness with regard to place and time—a sort of general oneness, if I may be allowed to use so strong an expression."

The President of the University is away in Persia and it is interesting to note that *en route* he went chasing all the way from London up to Scapa Flow to ask the Admiral of the Grand Fleet and his wife, *née* Marshall Field, to sign a legal document empowering the University to purchase a small alley-way which somehow stood in the way of the extension of the already ample University campus. In his absence we were hospitably entertained by his wife and the acting President.

We had a helpful conference during the afternoon with the Faculty in the Ida Noyes

Building, the home of the lady students,
but it is not fair to expect a lot of new-
comers to confer in a room decorated, as
this was, with the most charming of
modern frescoes. We couldn't help looking
at all the graceful and gorgeous young
creatures depicted in them and we were,
I fear, more interested in them than in the
exchange of Professors and Students. Why
can't we exchange frescoes? Later we
dined in the Hall of the same institution and
all made speeches.

Saturday, November 9th

To-day we journeyed through the
corn-fields and over the coal-fields to
Champagne-Urbana to visit the great Illinois State University—one of the biggest
and most rapidly growing of these institutions under State control. Stretching through
some forty-six of the forty-eight States,
with an aggregate of 175,000 students, these

State-aided Institutions are a power in the land. Their trustees are nominated by the Governor or the Mayor or are elected at the same time and by the same electoral body as the State legislature, and so little do they fear the interference of the politician that the President of one of the best-known of them said to us "they would feel kind of lonesome without it." After visiting the well-known horticultural branch of the University we were welcomed by addresses and other recitations, and tried to make suitable replies to some two or three thousand students and professors from a back-ground of four fair ladies representing respectively the United States, Illinois, Great Britain and Canada. In the evening we returned to Chicago.

Whilst we were away the Boy had been to a football match between Michigan and Chicago—Michigan won—and came back full of College yells.

Sunday, November 10th

We went a long drive along the North Shore and then visited the Academy of Fine Art. Amongst many priceless possessions is a whole room filled with Monets!

Monday, November 11th

"Peace hath murdered Sleep."

Hardly had we dozed off than we were awakened at 2 A.M. by a most infernal din. "Peace," as they will call an armistice, seemed to have been declared again. We were naturally sceptical, but being sceptical in bed whilst a million and a half were credulous outside doesn't bring sleep.

The noise was overwhelming. All that night and all next day and most of the next night the hooters hooted, the whistles whistled, the syrens syrened, brass utensils brayed, tin-trumpets trumpetted, the people yelled, the motors rushed about with tin-can accompaniments, boys banged bones, grown-up men frantically beat iron telegraph posts with crow-bars; every conceivable instrument was beaten, brayed or blown, but the hooters were the worst. They seemed to have an uncanny quality about them and as they moaned and boomed and shrieked they seemed to come into your room and you felt as though you could touch them. The parading people were excited, but good-natured and friendly. An elderly divine who took part in these nocturnal celebrations told us next morning that quite respectable ladies had put feathers down his neck; he added that after a time "one got quite used to it."

In the morning this noise increased. Thousands of lorries and motors pervaded the city packed with children and women, the latter by now beginning to look like Sisters of Mercy after a bump-supper. A peculiar manifestation of the enthusiasm of the people was the casting forth from every window innumerable scraps of paper—I believe the Telephone Directories suffered most—which blackened the skies and whitened the ground. It cost the City of New York $85,000 to clear up their paper litter after their dress-rehearsal last Thursday!

To-day we visited the North Western University. Like many others, it has certain of its Departments in the City, such as the Medical, the Commercial, the Dental, and the Legal. We had time only to visit the last two and found them well equipped and well staffed. There is even in the last-named a replica of a Law Court, and here the students try cases. I don't know whether I am more afraid of dentists or of lawyers; I suppose one is a physical and the other a moral fear, but I was glad to find myself on the way to Evanston, some twelve miles north of Chicago, where the main buildings of the North Western State

University are situate. Our progress was
impeded by parades; all the schools, all the
organized Societies paraded and all made
as much noise as they could. Finally,
however, we arrived at the Campus, beautifully placed on the shores of the lake. We
found here the same freshness of view, and
belief in the future, the same numerous
staff and adequate equipment that we had
found elsewhere; but there seems always
some novel and original feature in each
new institution we visit, and at the North
Western University we found a large
building entirely devoted to Oratory. Any
future Mission to this country, before embarking on its career of speeches, might
well take a short course of Oratory at
Evanston. After a comforting lunch at the
charming University Club, which was somewhat prolonged by all of us making speeches,
we returned to Chicago.

We dined this evening with the Association of the Presidents of State Universities.

I was so tired that, like the late Lord
Hartington, I nearly fell asleep during my
own speech and I could not help dozing
off again and again during those of my
colleagues. Each time I lost consciousness
I had a strange nightmare and it recurred
again and again. I dreamed that I had
heard it all before.

Tuesday, November 12th

It is difficult to recount the proceedings of last night, so I take refuge in an
excerpt from the sober columns of the
Tribune:

Delirium and license disputed the rule
of Chicago's streets last night. The mad
revel of the day approached an orgy last
night.

The wild celebration that had raged
since the darkness of the early morning
hours of Monday ended in hysteria in

the early morning hours of Tuesday.
Before midnight good natured rowdyism
had become general[1].

The members of the University Club
where we were lodged, whose hospitality is
boundless, gave us a sumptuous lunch in
their great dining-room which is a replica
of Crosby Hall seen under a magnifying
lens. The speeches were few, but good.

In the afternoon we attended a meeting
of the Presidents of State Universities and
amongst other good things heard a masterly
and witty address from the President of
Berkeley University.

Wednesday, November 13th

We left before eight in the morning
for Madison which is the capital of Wisconsin and the seat of one of the best-known and
most celebrated of the State Universities of

[1] *Chicago Daily Tribune*, 12. xi. 18.

the middle west. The University is set on a hill and a mile to the north on another hill the world-famed Capitol is set. The latter is built of a white granite, resembling marble. "The white Vermont (?) Marble used at Washington and elsewhere is a granite of medium grain; the constituents of which are normal in so far that they are quartz, mica and felspar. Generally, one or more of these constituents (most often the mica) are coloured—in this case all are colourless: the mica being quite colourless—probably muscovite." The building is cruciform and crowned by a dome as noble as that of St Paul's would be if the latter were cleaned; it is also a trifle higher.

Many of the professors hold executive positions under the Government and this happy combination of knowledge with statecraft seems to promote the welfare both of the commonwealth and of the University.

The weather was perfect, the sun blazing

hot and the air as crisp as Switzerland's. We went an enchanting drive along the shores of the two lakes, Mendota and Monona, which flank the two hills; their waters are as blue as those of the Grotto at Capri. We then attended a conference, important and heartening, but it hindered me from seeing all but the tail of a most brilliant sunset. The Boy saw it all and I was jealous.

We had a banquet with speeches in the evening in the spacious dining-room of the Madison Club where we are being housed. It is a delightful home and never have any of us revelled so much in perfect quiet and perfect views.

Thursday, November 14th

The Boy and I visited a few of the many Departments of the University, the Zoological, Botanical and Geological Laboratories, and those of the Institutes of Plant

Physiology and Plant Pathology. At Madison I saw the results of certain experiments which seemed to prove the inheritance of acquired characters, so often doubted. The experiments are not completed and, of course, there may be some flaw in the deductions, but to me they seemed conclusive, at any rate for the four generations which up till now form the basis of the experiment. After a delightful lunch at the Club we visited some of the many Departments of the College of Agriculture. After dining with the President of the University, we left for Minneapolis.

They do not pay in this country—or in any other—their Professors or their University Presidents enough. Perhaps it is because there are so many of them. At Universities not perceptibly larger than Cambridge the teaching staff is bigger than our whole Electoral Roll. The stipends of the teachers are as low as, in some cases even lower than, in Great Britain, and yet in normal times the expense of living is higher. Well it is the old, old story: "The cheapest thing going to-day," says the Satirist, "is education." "I pay my cook," said Crates, "four pounds a year; but a philosopher can be hired for about sixpence and a tutor for three-half-pence." "So to-day," writes Erasmus, "a man stands aghast at the thought of paying for his boy's education a sum which would buy a foal or hire a farm-servant." "Frugality! it is another name for madness!"

Friday, November 15th

At 10.30 A.M. we were received at the Minnesota State University, Minneapolis, at a Convocation held in the Armoury, no other building being large enough to seat the thousands who had come to welcome us. There were addresses, and three of us made speeches which were listened to with the utmost patience and sympathy, but the "note" of the ceremony was the music supplied by the Minneapolis Symphony Orchestra. This was really magnificent.

The Boy and I stayed with the President of the University and his family who, like all our hosts, were most kind in seeing that we had some sorely needed rest. In the late afternoon we had a very "nourishing" discussion with the Faculty and the executive officers and made a few short speeches after dining with them in the Ladies' Building.

Saturday, November 16th

I visited the Zoological Department and found amongst its many admirable features an aquarium half as large as that of the Marine Biological Association at Plymouth, a "beavery" where young beavers were building dams, and a Cinematograph Theatre fully equipped. The teachers make their own "movie" films. After a most pleasant luncheon with many of the Professors, the Boy went to a Wisconsin *v.* Minnesota football match. I did not, my attitude towards athletics being that of the Rhodes scholar whose certificate from his home University testified that "whilst he excelled in none he was sympathetic towards all."

In the evening a reception took place in our honour at the University President's House. We were introduced to, and shook hands with, some twelve hundred guests. This took some hours and the net result was that whilst our reason reeled, we seemed to have given pleasure to a great crowd of kindly folk; at any rate they were polite enough to say so.

Sunday, November 17ᵗʰ

In the morning I visited a famous private Art Collection with some wonderful Chinese curios and some fine pictures rather weakened by a number of quite mediocre paintings.

This city, though slightly south of Ottawa and Montreal and very slightly east of Des Moines,—it is on the 45° parallel,—is the most northerly and, until we reach Houston, Texas, the most westerly point of our journey. We now turn south and "nightly pitch our moving tent a day's march nearer home."

This afternoon I came across a couple of letters written by two Rulers on the same subject, but in different tones:

A *New York Times* correspondent sends from Paris the text of a letter written by the Kaiser to a German woman who has lost nine sons in the war. It is interesting, because of its contrast to the letter of President Lincoln to Mrs Bixby

during the American Civil War. The two letters
follow:

THE KAISER'S LETTER

His Majesty the Kaiser hears
that you have sacrificed nine
sons in defence of the Father-
land in the present war. His
Majesty is immensely gratified
at the fact, and in recognition
is pleased to send you his
photograph, with frame and
autograph signature.

LINCOLN'S LETTER

Dear Madam: I have been
shown in the files of the War
Department a statement of the
Adjutant General of Massachusetts that you are the mother
of five sons who have died
gloriously on the field of battle.
I feel how weak and fruitless
must be any words of mine
which should attempt to be-
guile you from the grief of a
loss so overwhelming. But I
cannot refrain from tendering
to you the consolation that
may be found in the thanks
of the Republic they died to
save. I pray that our Heavenly
Father may assuage the anguish
of your bereavement and leave
you only the cherished memory
of the loved and lost, and the
solemn pride that must be yours
to have laid so costly a sacri-
fice upon the altar of freedom.

In the evening we boarded the train for

Des Moines, Iowa. The first two or three hours were somewhat disturbed by the train developing a sort of rhythmic, mechanical hiccough on a large scale, but in time it found relief and we sleep.

Monday, November 18th

We were rather apprehensive about visiting Iowa, as some Iowans we had met in Minneapolis were so devoted to liberty that they seemed anxious to add to their own stock by taking it away from everyone else. However, Iowa turned out to be all right.

The object of our going to Des Moines was to visit the State College of Agriculture and Mechanic Arts at Ames, some thirty-five miles north of the Capital City. Here we split up into parties and I found it impossible to visit more than the Veterinary School and the Entomological Department. In the latter I went through part of a well-

known Collection of Mites and here I met
with the first instance I had ever come
across of a pathogenic organism conveyed
to a plant (the beetroot) by the bite of an
insect (a Leaf-hopper, *Eutettix tenella*
Baker). This "is the first plant disease
definitely determined to be entirely de-
pendent upon a specific insect for trans-
mission." Like the Yellow-fever pathogenic
organism, and apparently that which causes
the modern Influenza and many other of
our troubles, that of the "Curly-leaf-
disease" of Beets is ultra-microscopic.
The insect only conveys the disease if it
has fed upon a diseased beet, but a single
bite of an infected leaf-hopper will infect
the whole plant, and the disease only occurs
in the beet when bitten by this one species
of insect, and it takes two weeks after the
puncture to develop. Further, the insect is
not capable of conveying the disease at
once, it must have an incubation period
within the body of the insect of at least

twenty-four hours, often forty-eight. Thus this disease runs a course very similar to that of insect-borne protozoal diseases in animals. A somewhat similar history is now being worked out in a potato disease. These researches at Ames Agricultural College, Iowa, open up an entirely new field in plant pathology and will in all probability prove of the greatest economic value to the agriculturist.

The members of the Des Moines Club put us up during our stay in the Capital City and in the evening gave us one of the best dinners we had received in this land of dinners. We left them feeling as the tablets say in our re-decorated churches, "enlarged, restored and beautified," and making our way to the train, left for St Louis.

Tuesday, November 19th

The Chancellor and the authorities of the University, dedicated to the memory of that great Englishman, George Washington, at St Louis, were most considerate and, though placing themselves wholly at our disposal, left much of the time to ourselves. Washington University is finely situate on rising ground with spacious views, some five miles from the city. It is approached through a fine park, the site of the World's Fair in 1904. The entrance is both beautiful and imposing, a broad series of low steps leading up to the central gateway. All the buildings are planned by one architect, all are built of the same red granite—a local stone—and in the same style, so that here, even as much as at Chicago, the Campus has a unified charm rare in Western Universities. The Faculty gave us a sumptuous dinner, and although we said we would not make speeches, but would only just say "a word or two," at the end the Chancellor said he trembled to think what would have happened if we had made speeches.

Wednesday, November 20th

We spent the morning at the Medical
School and Hospital. These two institutions are practically one, and only some
four years old. Everything is of the best
and only to be equalled by such modern
temples of healing as that of the University
of Cincinnati, where, curiously enough, the
Mayor of the town appoints the members
of the Board of Regents. Such a complete
hospital with a medical school at its disposal, or such a complete medical school
with a hospital at its disposal—one does
not quite know which way to put it—is
unknown with us. Every patient can be
analysed, measured, rayed, tested, in fact
inspected with all the latest appliances of
science, and the medical student is trained
in all these processes; but when he becomes
the practising doctor in some small town
or remote village, what can he do in this
way even though (and this is never the

case) his patient could afford such refined treatment? Well, he must just do the best he can and must not envy the more fortunate folk at St Louis.

We are beginning to come across the problem of the coloured people. At Chicago black and white lie in the same wards, but at St Louis these patients do not mingle beyond the out-patient department, and farther south they do not mingle at all.

The black troops have fought gallantly. The Germans have complained about our fighting with coloured troops, but they have done far worse, they have been fighting with German troops. The other day a darkie soldier tried to break out of a camp in the South to see his folk, and after a lengthy dispute with the sentry, who told him he would be shot if he persisted, he replied, "Boss, t'ain' no sort o' use you stan'in' dere, 'cause I gwine *out*. I got a maw in Hebben an' I got a pa in Hell an' a sister in Memphis, an' I gwine see one of 'em dis night."

Later in the day we visited the Missouri Botanical Garden, presented and endowed by an Englishman, Mr Henry Shaw, who had made a large fortune in hardware. The gardens cover an area of 125 acres, and there are grown some 11,000 species of plants. The hot-houses are very fine, especially those devoted to heaths, orchids, cycads, palms and pineapples and the flora of the desert. One house was full of a Chrysanthemum show, the most interesting plant in which was the ur-chrysanthemum (*C. indicum* Linn.—partim—or *C. morifolium* Ram.), from which all modern forms are derived. It has an exceedingly beautiful though small blossom, and one could not but regret that the horticulturists had not left the lovely blossom alone, instead of breeding it into many-coloured monsters, which so singularly mimic their own paper imitations.

In the evening we left for Lexington, Kentucky.

Thursday, November 21st

Everywhere had we been received well and more than well, but at Lexington there was a warm-heartedness about our hosts which made us feel at once inhabitants of "My old Kentucky home." We motored out some twenty miles to the Shaker Village, where we fed on the dishes of the South, and very good dishes too, in a stately house with well-proportioned rooms, with a fine hall and ample staircase, and the date 1817 over the lintel of the front door. On the road we passed, what we had not passed before, the homes of country gentlemen who live in them, and do not merely sleep a "week-end" in them. Here they breed race-horses and race them, and raise tobacco and smoke it; in fact, Lexington is both a social and a trading centre.

This possibly accounts for the excellence of
the first-rate hotel where we were housed.

On returning we saw something of the
University buildings, and inspected the
Students' Army Training Corps, now all
eager to get out of khaki. At dinner we
were cheered by nigger minstrelsy and by
a minimum of speeches. Afterwards we
had a discussion with some of the Governors
and members of the Faculty. The value of
these discussions is always inversely pro-
portional to the size of the meeting. At
Lexington the meeting was small.

Friday, November 22nd

After a hurried visit to the University
Farm, where we were introduced to a hen
of unparalleled fecundity, and to the Schools
of Agriculture and Engineering, we left in
the morning for New Orleans, sorry to say
good-bye to Kentucky.

"The way of the transgressor is hard,"

said the coal-merchant to me as we sat in the minute smoking compartment of the observation car. "Last night," he continued, "I dissipated some, and all this morning I've been feeling mighty sick. Them folk that wrote the old Bible were smart, Sir, they knew all about human frailties, same as you and me."

I don't believe that I should have known that he was a coal-merchant but that he informed me that most folk liked to talk about what they traded in, and he talked about coal. He took a profound interest in a pile of coal at one of the depots we halted at. To me it seemed much the same as any other coal-dump, and it only appealed to me as a rather lavish display of what in my country is a really rare mineral. The sight of a funnel or chute for conveying the coal into the trucks excited his enthusiasm. I suppose there was some money-saving contrivance in it which attracted him, but I confess, whatever it was, it left me cold.

All the day and all the night we traversed

Kentucky, Tennessee, Alabama, Mississippi, until on—

Saturday, November 23rd

we pulled about noon into the
depot at New Orleans. Most of the
morning we had been crossing great arms
of the sea, old mouths of the Mississippi,
but now known as Lake Pontchartrain, or
skirting inland waterways, bayous. One
wished we could see a crocodile.

After all, there are only two species of
crocodile in North America, and one of these
is an alligator. We couldn't possibly see
the true crocodile (*Crocodilus americanus*
Laurenti) as, though it extends from central
Mexico to Equador and the West Indian
Islands, in the States it lives only in the
waterways and the salt water marshes of the
southern tip of Florida. It is an agile, vicious
beast but no man-eater. More slender than
the alligator and with a pointed snout, it is

much more active and swift in its movements. Its colour changes as it ages, but there is always more olive-green and gray in its pigmentation than in that of the alligator. It was discovered only in 1875. "Oh! What a crocodilian year was that!" as Francis Quarles exclaims in his *Emblems*. Quarles was a member of my College, Christ's!

The last-named (*Alligator mississippiensis* (Daudin)) has more yellow and black patches and a broader head and snout. It is usually said that its growth is slow, but Ditmars' observations show that the growth in length and in weight is comparatively rapid. This alligator extends from North Carolina to Florida and as far west as the Rio Grande in Texas, frequenting the low swamps and rivers of the coast. Unfortunately it is becoming extinct and the discovery that its skin can be tanned and made into leather for bags and purses is hastening its disappearance. Two and a

half million were destroyed in the years
1880–1894 chiefly for their skins. In the
south their eggs are also eaten, for, unfortunately for the race, alligators lay very
palatable eggs and their nests are conspicuous and easily rifled.

Alone amongst reptiles the alligator
roars. Other reptiles hiss but the 'gator, as
the coloured folk call him, emits a bellow
which in the still night of the south carries
a mile or more. The voice of the young is
as the "mooing" of a cow, but a big male,
ten feet or more in length, roars with a
thunderous and tremulous blast. He, at
the same time, emits from under his chin
"fine steaming jets of a powerful nasty
smelling fluid" which "float off into the
heavy miasmatic atmosphere of the bayou."
The odour may be carried for miles and to
the negroes it always signifies "a big ol'
'gator."

On arriving at the Depot at New Orleans
we left immediately for Tulane University

and *en route* some of us must have fallen in with a reporter. Hitherto I have shown a certain reticence about the members of our Commission, but now all is discovered!

The New Orleans Item has given us away, given us away rather too generously. I quote from its classic columns:

BRITISH EDUCATORS VISIT NEWCOMB WITH DINWIDDIE

"TUBBING" IS PART OF BRITISHERS' PRELIMINARIES FOR TOUR OF CITY

The British University Mission—which was heralded as the British Education Mission, an error, as the members have to do only with college and university work—arrived in New Orleans, Saturday shortly after noon, and after a short stay at the Grünewald for the "tubbing," which constitutes as much of British formality as any of their other national customs, were driven to Tulane University by Capt. Edith Haspel and Corporal Flower of the Emergency Motor Corps of the American Red Cross.

"Oh, I say," said Sir H—— J——, seeing the Red Cross insignia on the cap of Captain Haspel, "You're not going to take us to a hospital? What?"

But it was to Newcomb that the party of British educators went after a short stay at the hotel. Dr Dinwiddie of Tulane and Dr Pierce Butler of Newcomb met the party at the station and accompanied the five members of the mission to a luncheon that had been arranged, prepared and served by members of the domestic science class of Newcomb College.

"Chilly, Eh Wot?"

As the automobile sped up St Charles avenue, Reverend E—— W——, Fellow and Tutor of

8—2

Queen's College, Oxford, Member of the Heb-
domadal History (*sic*), leaned close to Dr J——
J——, Professor of Geology and Mineralogy,
Trinity College, Dublin, and said:

"It's beastly chilly, Eh Doctor?"

"Quite so, my dear Doctor, I had expected a
much milder climate something like Capri,
what?"

"Righto!"

Dr Dinwiddie explained that this was severe
weather for the early winter, but the disappointment was evident in Dr W——'s face. It is the
winter, but the disappointment of the doctor's
first trip to America, and his impressions are
varied.

"I rather expected to see life of a more tropical
nature," he said, "are there no fruits at this time
of year, no bananas? I had expected to see
monkeys, and other tropical animals here—I am
quite disappointed, you know!"

New Orleans Item.
25. xi. 18.

"SOLDIER LOSES BUTTON"

Sir A—— S——[1] has with him a Secretary, a young English soldier, blue-eyed, blond[2] and big. Shivers of excitement were noticed among the girls of Newcomb when he appeared among the older members of the Mission. But Lieut. N—— was worried. "I'm in a deuce of a predicament," he said, "I've lost a button from my uniform and it makes me feel so undressed, you know—"

"Suppose," said Dr Dinwiddie, "that we have one of the young ladies sew it on for you."

"I should be most pleased," said Lieutenant N——, and presently he was led away in quest of a needle, thread and a girl[3] attached.

"Isn't it odd," said Dr S—— when Lieut. N—— returned beaming with the glint of an international romance in his blue eye, "I, too, have lost a button!"

[1] The kindly Southerner often grants honours which are quite unmerited.

[2] He has black hair and dark eyes but something must be sacrificed to alliteration.

[3] A friendly negress of mature charms.

We lunched as usual in the Ladies' College, called after Miss H. S. Newcomb. We saw something of the several departments, and in that of Household Economy I had just time to copy from the blackboard some recipes for salads, oyster-cocktails, and other comforts before being hurried along to chemistry. Whilst eating the admirable "gumbo," a sort of bouille-abaisse but less fishy, prepared by the students, I congratulated myself that I had done so. We made a few speeches, and were especially interested in one by the Dean of Newcomb Hall, and one by the Professor of Engineering who was trained at Annapolis, and told us of the part our Admiralty had played in training the men who built up the American Navy.

The Art School at Newcomb College is outstanding. The Director is a gifted artist. As in many other American Universities, ceramics take a leading part in the art students course, but embroidery, church

vestments, metal work, and jewellery are
also studied, besides painting and modelling.
A student with a taste for any of the so-
called "Arts and Crafts" can pay her way
through College after her sophomore year
and has no difficulty in making a living
after graduating. Indeed, the Dean of
Newcomb College told us he could "place"
double the number of graduates were the
College twice as big.

We are on the 30 parallel, well south of
the Canary Islands and of Cairo, yet it is
cold, bleak and, worst of all, wet. In spite
of this, I was able to see enough of the city
to prove in my eyes it is the most beautiful
of the many cities I have visited in the
United States during the last thirty-two
years. The wonderful avenues with grass
down the middle, and palms down the sides,
the luxurious gardens which form a setting
for the houses of the well-to-do, all open
to the public gaze, make a whole which,
to one with a soul inclining as Lowell

says "to the southern slope," is irresistible.

We dined with the President of Tulane and heard some charming negro melodies, mostly of the revivalist sort. Just now "negro-spirituals" are the fashion, especially in the North.

Some of the experiences of the darkie at the Front are striking. A bunch of correspondents there came across a big black Corporal suffering from the effects of high explosives and asked what they could do to help." Well, suh, boss, I don' jess rightly know whut ail me. Well, suh, yeh know, dee sawnt us up yonder a little piece. We wus dere fur two days wid dem big shells jess bustin' up de town: and dee had tole us to git under kiver when er shell come. Well, suh, boss, I wus out dere, an' de shells commence ter come an' I went fer to git under kiver. Mos' all de houses wus gone, blowed plumb down; but I seen one dese here places whut dee calls a Tav*ern*—

you know, boss, dat means er saloon. Dey wa'n't no folks in hit, but I jess made up my min' I wus gwine git in dat house. An' I reach out my han' fer de door knob. An' jess when I gits ready to open de do'— Blim—Blim—Blooy—here come er shell an' jess tuck dat saloon out uv my han'."

During the evening we had an informal talk at the Round Table Club and here we met many interesting and leading citizens of New Orleans. The President of Tulane is a man of few words, but has a remarkable power of hitting a nail on the head. He certainly made us think as he pointed out certain snags in our way.

Sunday, November 24ᵗʰ

To-day was glorious, bright sun-shine and clear air. The Boy and I visited the French quarter and found it picturesque but decayed. It simply exuded romance and obviously we must all read George Cable's stories all over again. We attended a service at the Cathedral and then sat in the sun and were daguerreotyped, and had a group of piccaninnies similarly treated. I had thought this was a dead art, but it isn't, and it was delightful to see the old daguerreotypist fishing our pictures on little metal plates by means of a magnet out of a pail with some solution in it. The little darkies guessed we were French and then Italian, and their powers of speculation being by now exhausted, we told them that we were English. Immediately they took the Boy to be the Prince of Wales and guessed he was mighty glad to be out of that battle and assured us that they would have felt the same in similar circumstances. We also visited the fruit market, a riot of colour.

In the afternoon we attended a conference in the Gold Room of our Hotel, the most charming feature of which was the beautiful singing of our lady hostesses.

In the evening we left in a private car for Houston, Texas.

Monday, November 25th

My *Cambridge Pocket Diary* records that to-day the "Inns of Court Michaelmas (Dining) Term ends." Such a statement makes one feel homesick. It is so essentially English. Surely in no other country in the world could such an event happen. Principalities and powers are tottering, crowns are crashing and the "Inns of Court Michaelmas (Dining) Term ends" on the normal date.

The weather adds to our nostalgia for it is foggy, wet and cold, not at all the weather for the Hispano-moresque buildings of the Rice Institution (by Cram) which demand a blazing sun and blue sky.

They are indeed wonderful buildings and
recalled Browning's lines:

> A sort of temple—perhaps a college,
> —Like nothing I ever saw before
> At home in England, to my knowledge.
>
> *Christmas Eve and Easter Day.*

After a formal reception in the Faculty
Chamber we lunched with the Mayor and
Municipality at the huge Rice Hotel, which
would be conspicuous even in New York.
Houston is a comparatively new city but
its enterprise is boundless. In the afternoon
I gave a lecture to a crowded audience on
"The Depths of the Sea." The hearers
were very patient and very appreciative.

We are staying in a most charming house,
one of the most comfortable I have ever been
in, and one feels absolutely at home but with
superadded comforts. The flowers alone
are a joy after days of flowerless hotels and
trains. In the evening there was a reception
and here we met the Governor of the State

and many others with whom we had all too little time to talk.

Tuesday, November 26th

Conferences and lectures took up much of the day but their rigour was mitigated by a luncheon given us by the Chamber of Commerce. I always like talking to business men; somehow they seem more easily pleased than their academic brothers.

The food controller of Texas gave a stimulating address on the success of the efforts made in this respect in the State, and some striking statistics of the food shortage which still obtains throughout the Old World. A well-attended smoking concert at the roomy University Club, with more short addresses, closed a somewhat strenuous day.

Wednesday, November 27th

All the morning we held a series of discussions and conferences on a "League

of Nations," a "Federation of Churches,"
a "League of Learning." No one will
clearly define what the suggested "League
of Nations" is to be, and no one will tell
us if the Central Powers of Europe are to
be leaguers or not. After all, no one knows
whether there will be many nations in
what was Russia or many in what was
Germany, so the discussion is a little premature. Still, a good many find the phrase,
as the old lady found the word Mesopo-
tamia, helpful and soothing.

We lunched at the invitation of the City
Board of Education at the South End
Junior High School. The Republic of
Texas (1836–48) split off from the mother
country Mexico for many reasons; one, and
this is surely unique amongst rebelling
States, was that the Central Government
did not supply the people with sufficient
public schools. This deficiency is now made
good, but generous as the tax-payer is to
education, it is difficult to keep pace with

the growth of the people and the deep-
rooted determination to educate their
children. The school where we found ourselves was a fine building standing in
spacious grounds. Inside were wide corri-
dors, ample staircases, well-proportioned
class-rooms, a magnificent gymnasium and
swimming bath. The care of the body is
only second, perhaps not always second,
to the care of the mind in American schools
and colleges.

Thursday, November 28th

Thanksgiving Day.

And very real thanksgivings were given
on this most memorable day. A spirit of
rest and relief was in the land. We have
been over here just fifty days, we have
visited about fifty Universities, we have
travelled some five thousand miles, and
have met some fifty thousand professors,
or so it seemed to me, and we were tired

and rather New-World-worn. Hence we accepted the kind invitation of our more than kind host and took a couple of days off. We were rewarded and our proceeding was sanctioned by the weather, for we had a typical Texan day, a warm sun, a cool but not cold day, and a cloudless blue sky.

The officers of the 57th Regiment invited me to a dinner and dance they were giving to the General in command. It was an admirably managed affair. The meal was served on long tables set around the ball-room and between each course the young people danced to the music of the regimental band. I felt quite like an ancient Roman.

Sydney Smith used to say that the highest form of human happiness was "eating paté-de-foie gras to the sound of trumpets." I have never tried this, but I feel convinced that eating pineapple-salad to the dance music of the 57th Regiment's band makes a very good second.

Friday, November 29th

After fixing up our tickets for the journey to Boston I had time to visit the hospital at the Logan Camp. The wards are "open air" and the abundance of mosquito wiring was evidence of a trouble from which we at home are almost free. The kitchen, with every conceivable device to save labour, was spotlessly clean and owing to a native skill in cooking and an abundance of most varied foods, the patients are better fed than with us.

We felt sorry to leave Houston. Our hosts were kind beyond measure. They all conspired to make us feel we were not guests but members and popular members of the family, and they fully succeeded. We were sorry to leave "the darkies," they were so willing to help and so anxious to oblige. As they told our hostess, they knew at once we were English because they could not understand a single word we said.

Their smile and general cheerfulness deserve
many marks. Their philosophy ought to
teach us a lesson. One who was asked why
negroes never commit suicide replied,
"Well, Boss, it's jes' lik' dis—White man
sit down an' worries about his troubles till
he jes' goes an' shoots hisself. Niggah sit
down and worries about his troubles an'
jes' nachally fall asleep." Surely the better
way.

Saturday, November 30th

St Andrew's Day.

We traversed half of Texas in the night,
and part of Louisiana; at New Orleans we
changed trains and Depots early in the
morning and then we traversed Mississippi.
Until we had left Mobile we were never
far from the Gulf, and we were passing
through scenery like that of the everglades
of Florida. We saw innumerable sluggish
waterways, with turbid, almost stagnant,

streams with low muddy banks, the flat
land clothed with a tangle of sub-tropical
vegetation, the trees, never large, bearded
with streamy lichens, "Spanish-moss" as
the term goes, stood out of a matted im-
penetrable undergrowth still green but so
tired-looking! Except for the buzzards,
which are ubiquitous, we saw little or no
bird life.

Alabama provided us with such a sunset
as I have never before seen, not even in
South Africa or in Egypt. A vast continent
of molten gold, with opal lakes and inlets
of the sea, and here and there black patches
like cities set on their shores. No words
can describe it. Some one placed "in a
golden chair" had splashed "at a ten-league
canvas with brushes of comets' hair." It
lasted fully an hour, but only the Boy and
the Knight and I watched it. Its glory was
concealed from our fellow-travellers who
for most part slumbered and slept.

Sunday, December 1st

On a Pullman car one learns much about the legislation of the several States. The varying injunctions are printed on the bills-of-fare and suggest fertile subjects of conversation with one's fellow-travellers. For instance, it is forbidden in Tennessee and in Indiana to sell cigarettes. Apparently one may buy them and the tobacco shops are open and flourish, but their sale is forbidden. We kept east of Tennessee and were quite a long way off Indiana. In Georgia the Legislature has forbidden all tipping, but we only passed through a corner of Georgia and the kindly railway authorities, ever mindful of the welfare of their dining-car waiters, had so arranged the time-table that we passed through this corner between meals.

When I first arrived in New York, thirty-two years ago, I put up at the Windsor Hotel, long since burned down. Tipping was not very prevalent in those days. There was a kind of attitude of a people "too proud" to tip, though I have never actually met anyone who refused to take one. Still, you didn't tip the men who looked after your hat whilst you were dining. These were very wonderful men. They gave you no check, and as you left the dining-room they prided themselves on handing you back the right hat. Coming out just before me a gentleman received a hat which made him exclaim: "That's not my hat!" "I don't know whether it's your hat or not," said the hat man, "it's the hat you g've me!" Nowadays you very soon spend the cost of your hat in gratifying the hat-guardians if you lunch or dine in restaurants or hotels at all frequently.

You now receive a check but the checking is not so accurate as the hatmen of the 'eighties. Coming away the other day after lunch one heard a fellow-luncher saying to his companion, "What on earth did you give that fellow ten dollars for?" "Well, look at that coat he has given me," was the response, as the happy tipper exhibited a five-hundred dollar fur-lined coat.

All through Georgia and the two Carolinas the cotton crops were awaiting picking. What with one thing and another the harvest down south lasts half the year. We passed a number of modern cotton factories engaged, as the conductor told us, in the manufacture of "domestics." At Lynchburg, Va., we bought some persimmons, but eating persimmons is to "snatch a fearful joy" and we soon desisted.

Monday, December 2nd

Owing to engine trouble we were late in reaching Washington; however we did get there between 2 and 3 A.M., and found the city, on the eve of the President's farewell address, fast asleep. During the morning we went shopping, saw some old friends and some Senators. No matter where they come from, Senators seem to acquire a certain "facies" as zoologists term it, something between that of a popular preacher and an important tragedian. They are readily recognised by a systematist.

We visited the enormous grounds of the Bureau of Standards, covered with countless laboratories in which every conceivable article used by the Government is tested and analysed. We also saw the well-equipped Zoological Gardens, open free to all, maintained "by the people and for the people."

In the evening we left for Boston, our fourth consecutive night on the cars.

Tuesday, December 3rd

We were put up again in our old home at Cambridge by the ever hospitable President of Harvard and his kindly wife, and were delighted to find there was for one day nothing particular to do, and in the words of the poet we "did it very well."

Wednesday, December 4th

This morning we attended the twentieth Annual Meeting of the "Association of American Universities" which consists of the Presidents and certain of the Deans of the several Universities. It is perhaps the most important educational body we met, and the discussions in which we took part were on a high level. In the evening we were hospitably entertained at the Harvard Club.

The witty and good-humoured "sparring" between the Presidents of two of the oldest American Universities called to my mind in an inverted sort of way a conversation between two wealthy New Yorkers, both of whom were wedded to wives with social ambitions. "Is your wife entertaining this season?" said one to the other, about Christmas time; "Not very," was the sad reply.

Thursday, December 5th

Neither the Boy nor I have quite got over our four days' continuous trip from Texas to Massachusetts. He has been writing and reading most of the time and revelling in certain rare early editions of Edgar Allan Poe which he has found in the Harvard University Library. I have felt so tired that to-day I stopped in bed until tea-time. I feel as Pinkerton did, "I want to lie on my back in a garden and read Shakespeare and E. P. Roe," only it's snowing outside.

This meeting of the "Association of American Universities" is the last item of our official programme and we rather characteristically brought our Mission to an end by cutting a Session of the Deans in the evening. It was snowing heavily out-of-doors and we stopped at home—for it is a home—turned down the lights and told ghost stories.

This seems a suitable date to close this diary. We shall have, by the time we reach home, travelled about twice the diameter of the earth, and everywhere we have met friends, and nearly everywhere we had fine weather, for the heavens smiled on our Mission.

A highland minister, a mystic and a man of blameless life, went out to the Front as "padre" to a regiment largely recruited from his district. He was one of those unhappy mortals who believed that for him there was no hope. Every now and then he could not refrain from seeking human sympathy, and one day, pouring out his troubles to a blue-eyed subaltern, he ended his discourse by saying, "I veritably believe I am the wickedest man in France." "Yes Sir," said the boy, "but you must remember what a deuce of a good time you must have had."

I think we shall all go back to our country

remembering "what a deuce of a good time" we have had.

And here, if I may quote the words of the unknown author of the Maccabees:

And here will I make an end,

And if I have done well, and as is fitting the story, it is that which I desired, and if slenderly and meanly, it is that which I could attain unto....And as wine mingled with water is pleasant and delighteth the taste, even so speech, finely framed, delighteth the ears of them that read the story.

And here shall be an end.

F I N I S

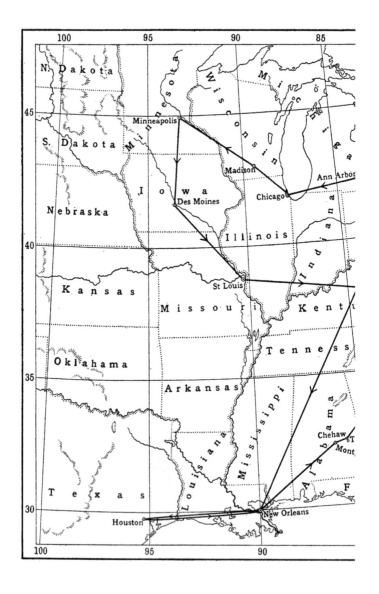

For EU product safety concerns, contact us at Calle de José Abascal, 56–1°, 28003 Madrid, Spain or eugpsr@cambridge.org.

www.ingramcontent.com/pod-product-compliance
Ingram Content Group UK Ltd.
Pitfield, Milton Keynes, MK11 3LW, UK
UKHW020314140625
459647UK00018B/1868